T0368451

Sadie-

Linda Moody

Inspirational

Poetry

AuthorHouse™
1663 Liberty Drive
Bloomington, IN 47403
www.authorhouse.com
Phone: 833-262-8899

Because of the dynamic nature of the Internet, any web addresses or links contained in this book may have changed
since publication and may no longer be valid. The views expressed in this work are solely those of the author and do not
necessarily reflect the views of the publisher, and the publisher hereby disclaims any responsibility for them.

Any people depicted in stock imagery provided by Getty Images are models,
and such images are being used for illustrative purposes only.
Certain stock imagery © Getty Images.

This book is printed on acid-free paper.

ISBN: 979-8-8230-3639-9 (sc)
ISBN: 979-8-8230-3641-2 (hc)
ISBN: 979-8-8230-3640-5 (e)

Library of Congress Control Number: 2024922154

Print information available on the last page.

Published by AuthorHouse 10/21/2024

authorHOUSE®

Barfield

"Family reunion"

B is for benevolence, loves everyone around

A is for amiable, kindhearted at all times;

R is for rigid, strict and firm,

F is for faith, trust, believed that you will win

I is for insight, the gift of discerning one's life,

E is for excel, without envy and strife;

L is for lending, grant a helping hand,

D is for determine, willing to stand;

cc:2007
Sadie L. Moody

Yield To The King

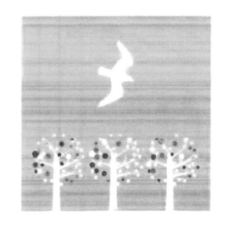

The year of economic crisis is almost here
And the end of time is approaching near.
Many are troubled about the future event:
God wants us to relax and be content.

This world is drowning in discouragement and uncertainty:
Many have lost control of their destiny.
There is hope in discouraging times:
God is going to turn things around.

Remember. God is the one in control:
For He knows what the future holds.
Surely. we are facing a difficult test:
God is yet over the whole universe:

So as the spirit of God moves in our midst:
We know for certain God still exists.
So yield to the King as never before:
Soon these days we will see no more.

cc:2007
Sadie Moody

"Now. be ye not stiff necked. as your Fathers were. but yield
yourselves unto the Lord. and enter into his sanctuary. which
he hath sanctified forever: and serve the Lord your God that
the fierceness of his wrath may turn away from you."
II Chronicles 30:8

PEER PRESSURE

Do not be misled: "Bad company corrupts good character" I Corin. 15:33

Baby

A Miracle From God

A miracle from God to call our own
Our hearts are rejoicing in this home
Such a little one to cherish and adore
We couldn't ask God for anything more

We're blessed with the very best
A new life brought into our nest
Our days are filled with joy and pleasure
Thank God for such
a gift to treasure

Sadie Moody 1998©

There shall be showers of blessings.
Ezekiah 34:26

Anxiety

Trust God and Overcome Anxiety

Go to God in prayer and confident
Allow Him to guard
your heart and mind
In every situation always be content
In Him peace will surely find

Keep your mind on God
as never before
Let your belief and
sincerity be evident
Rejoice in Him forever more
It does not matter to what extent

Sadie Moody ©1998

Be careful for nothing; but in everything be prayer and supplication
with Thanksgiving let your requests be made known unto God.
And the peace of God, which passeth all understanding, shall
keep your hearts and minds through Christ Jesus.

Philippians 4:6-7

The Church

Whenever God builds a church,
And it's built on prayer
The devil will always
Try to set up a chapel there.

God Is Declaring Judgment To This Rebellious Nation

Injustice is festering and so is greed
And people haven't taken heed
Businesses are blooming and boundaries are bulging
There's more and more sins people are indulging

True worship has been replaced with hypocritical
religious motions
God desires our entire life and not just a portion;
He's trying to mobilize this nation to repent;
That we may visualize the nearness of his judgment

In this world there is so much contesting,
Many people all over this world are stressing
God's Prophet cries out for righteousness and justice
In order that the people may receive peace

Famine, floods, drought and plagues are going to bring us
to our knees
Because of the directions this nation is headed, God is not
pleased
Remember, God always send a prophet who lashes out at
sins unflinchingly
One who speaks with power, authority and intensity

Amos: 3:1—6:14   Sadie Moody [cc:Feb. 2011]

It's Time To Resort To The Solitude Of The Mountains And Pray

There is no doubt, God will meet you there,
Communion with God will ennoble the
Character of your life
Release from your heart envy, jealousy, and strife.

In order to receive spiritual refreshing;
Continue seeking God until you receive his blessing.
We should always take the time and be set apart.
Be honest sincere from the depths of your heart.

So be ready in the morning, and come up in the morning to Mount Sinai, and present yourself to me there on the top of the Mountain. And no man shall come up with you, and let no man be seen throughout all the mountain, let neither flocks nor herds feed before that mountain.
Exodus 34:2-3

CC Sadie Moody
2/2010

God's Chosen Deacon

Commissioned by the Apostle as he laid hands
He has the reputation of a good man
Full of wisdom and the Holy Ghost
Helps in the ministry whereever needed most

One who seeks God and really prays
Continually praying each and every day
When the Apostle preaches and the people are being fed
He's always witnessing "Amen" to God's word

He looks into the ministry spiritual oversight
That no one would be left slight
In all that he does blameless he was found
Even when no one else was around

Sadie Moody   ©2000

*For they that have used the office of a deacon well purchase to themselves
a good degree, and great boldness in the faith which is in Christ Jesus.
I Timothy 3:13*

December

The Suffering Of One's Life

In this life, we will go through;
Our suffering helps us to endure,
The tests and trials may seem hard;
But our promises are great rewards

We sometimes suffer for being misused;
Other times, when being false accused,
When we suffer for righteousness sake
God is teaching us how to take

(Romans 8:18)
For I reckon that the sufferings of this present time are not worthy to be compared
with the glory which shall be revealed in us.

Poetry: By Sadie L. Moody
Sermon: Preached by Douglas Sutton
(cc: 2008)

13

Fret Not God
Is
With Thee

Fret not because of the evil doer
One day they will become the battle loser
They walk to and fro day by day
Biting against you in every way

Within their heart lies envy and strife
The words they speak cut as a knife
Sowing discord is one thing God hate
You will not be able to enter His gate

Some falsely accuse you with all their might
Knowing a liar shall not tarry in God's sight
The seeds they sow will come back around
Faint not, God will take care in due time

Psalm 21:11 - For they intended evil against thee: they imagined a
mischievous device, which they are not
able to perform.

Sadie Moody   cc:2001

Grieve Not The Holy Spirit

If a servant of God is grieved
They will suffer much sorrow
In God they yet believe
But, fears the tests of tomorrow

The pains of grieving come to destroy
And a wounded spirit becomes in distress
They sometimes even lose their joy
And many nights obtain little rest

Grieve not the Holy Spirit
Because the spirit of God grieves too
All that happens God can fix it
And He knows just what to do

Sadie Moody
© 1997

Ephesians 4:30
And grieve not the holy Spirit of God,
whereby ye are sealed unto the day of redemption.

Yellow Brick Road ©96

16

Desires of Your Heart

Obey God's commandments in

the fullness and not in part,

He will meet every need

And give you the desires of your heart

Rest in Him in all you do

There's nothing He will withhold from you,

Trust him and obey

He will certainly make a way

Sadie Moody
© 1997

Deuteronomy 11:24
"Every place whereon the soles of your feet
shall tread shall be yours;
from the wilderness and Lebanon,
from the river, Euphrates,
even unto the uttermost sea shall your coast be."

Remember Time is Valuable

Make the most of today because, time is passing by.
Treasure every moment you have.
Share your miracles and your
blessings with someone else.
To realize the value of one year, ask a student
who failed a grade
To realize the value of one month, ask a mother
who gave birth to a premature baby
To realize the value of one week, ask the
editor of a weekly newspaper
To realize the value of one hour, ask the person
who prayed for one hour
To realize the value of one minute, ask a person
who missed the train
To realize the value of one millisecond,
ask the person
who won a silver medal in the Olympics
"Time waits for no one"
Yesterday is history
Tomorrow is a mystery
Today is for sharing time
Share your valuable time and be blessed.

Sadie Moody
©1998

18

The Gossiper

Always telling something you heard
Saying they said, he said, she said, and it said
Not knowing the truth about the matter
But with your lips they always flatter

Stop being a talebearer, and strife will cease
Because God requires all of us to follow peace
When lying on others, it causes ruin
Conversation that's not of God, we should shun

Hating on others causes strife;
Ugly words spoken cut as a knife,
Be careful what you say or do,
Because God's seeing eyes are watching you.

The words of a talebearer are as wounds, and they go down into the inner most parts of the belly.
A lying tongue hateth those that are afflicted by it; and a flattering mouth worketh ruin.
Proverbs 26:22,28

Cc: 2009
Sadie L. Moody

A Strong Soldier

A very very strong soldier you are
You've kept the faith thus far
Continued steadfast in the Lord
When the battle was very hard

You believed God would bring you out
Trusted Him and did not doubt
You stood very strong
When it seemed all was going wrong

Many couldn't see nor understand
But you knew what God had planned
Always calling on God in prayer
Knowing that He would meet you there.

Sadie Moody
©1998

I Peter 5:10

*But the God of all grace, who
hath called us unto his eternal glory
by Christ Jesus, after that ye have
suffered a while, make you perfect,
stablish, strengthen, settle you.*

Sadie Moody

Trust God and Overcome Anxiety

Go to God in prayer and confident
Allow Him to guard your heart and mind
In every situation always be content
In Him peace will surely find

Keep your mind on God as never before
Let your belief and sincerity be evident
Rejoice in Him forever more
It does not matter to what extent

Sadie Linda Moody
© 1998

Philippians 4:6-7
Be careful for nothing; but in everything by
prayer and supplication with Thanksgiving let
your requests be made known unto God.
And the peace of God, which passeth all understanding,
shall keep your hearts and minds through Christ Jesus.

Encouragement

You Can Go Through The Wilderness

In the wilderness there's a highway
You can walk through everyday
God will make the crooked road straight
There you will be able to enter into the gate

Through every wilderness and mountain you shall go
All of the high hills will be made low
Every rough place God will make plain
There you will be able to explain

He'll open the rivers in high places
You can rejoice through each one you face
He'll give a pool of water in the wilderness
That you will not be able to resist.

Sadie Moody
1997 ©

Isaiah 35:1
The wilderness and the solitary place
shall be glad for them; and the desert
shall rejoice, and blossom as the rose.

The Glory of the Lord

When God's glory comes into our midst,
We'll know that His spirit does exist
As a light proceeds to and fro
Deliverance will come as we know.

His spirt shall come upon thee
All sickness and diseases must flee
In our minds we'll have no doubt
Because we'll know what it's all about

His Glory is in our midst

© Sadie Moody 1997

Haggai 2:9
The glory of this latter house shall be greater than of the former,
saith the Lord of host; and in this place will I give peace, saith the Lord of hosts.

Isaiah 60:1
Arise, shine; for thy light is come, and the glory of the Lord is risen upon thee.

Father's Day

The Man of Faith

He walks by faith and not by sight,
He yet knows that God will make everything all
right,
In his family, difficult times may come;
Not knowing where their blessings are coming
from;

But, he believes God and stand strong in faith,
A man that have learned how to take;
Regardless to what the enemy tries to do,
God will be there to see him through

Sadie L Moody
cc: 2006

II Corinthians 5:7; (For we walk by faith, not by sight)

THE HUSBAND OF UNDERSTANDING

A husband that will never harbor the thought that
their marriage is a mistake,
For he will learn how to forgive and take;

He encourages his wife when fighting the battles of
life,
Because the enemy tries to bring envy and strife;

Always seeks to stand by her side,
Allowing God to direct and be their guide;

Then, instead of the marriage ending,
Their love will be as the very beginning

Sadie L. Moody
cc:2006

:

The Pulpit Warmers

When the pulpit warmers become slack
Seeking God's face is one thing they lack
They seldom pray for the Pastor to lead
But tries to overtake and tell other to take
heed

They seldom tend to say "Amen" to God's word
While the Pastor preach and the people are
being fed
They have no eye to see nor ears to hear
What God's spirit is saying to them

The Pastor really needs people who will pray
And pray continually each and everyday
Not Sundays only, when everyone is a round
But during their sickness and trial times

Sadie L. Moody cc:2008

The Glory of the Lord

When God's glory comes into our midst,
We'll know that His spirit does exist
As a light proceeds to and fro
Deliverance will come as we know.

His spirit shall come upon thee
All sickness and diseases must flee
In our minds we'll have no doubt
Because we'll know what it's all about
HIS GLORY IS IN OUR MIDST

© Sadie Moody 1997

Haggai 2:9
The glory of this latter house shall be greater than of the former,
saith the Lord of host; and in this place will I give peace, saith the Lord of hosts.

Isaiah 60:1
Arise, shine; for thy light is come, and the glory of the Lord is risen upon thee.

The Rainbow Sign

God showed Noah the rainbow

Just as it appeared in the sky

He assured Noah as we know

That the world would be

destroyed by fire.

Sadie Moody
©1998

Genesis 9:13
I do set my bow in the clouds and it shall
be for a token of a covenant between me and the earth.

What ever you plant, will surely grow. Be careful about the seed you sow.

Job 4:8, Even as I have seen, they that plow iniquity, and sow wickedness, reap the same.

I will not allow criticism, circumstances, or disappointments to determine who I am. For I am a child of the king

Galatians 4:7-Wherefore thou art no more a servant, but a son; and if a son, then an heir of God through Christ.

cc2008 Sadie L. Moody

Loves conquers all.
Let us also learn to
love and yield to love
and not hate

I John 4: 7-8
Everyone who loves is born of God and knows
God. He that loveth not knoweth not God; for
God is love

Sadie L. Moody cc: 2008

Associate yourself with people of good character if you value your own reputation. It is better to be alone than in the company of evil doers

Sadie L. Moody cc: 2008

Pray for
what you
want, but
work for the
things you need.

Sadie Moody ©1998

Wealth gotten by vanity shall be diminished:
but he that gathereth by labor shall increase.
Proverbs 13:11

Pray for what you want, but work for the things you need.

Sadie Moody ©1998

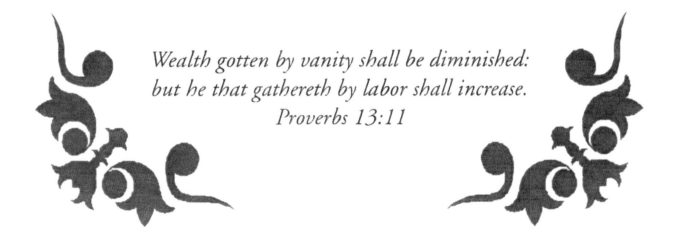

Wealth gotten by vanity shall be diminished:
but he that gathereth by labor shall increase.
Proverbs 13:11

You Can Go Through The Wilderness

In the wilderness there's a highway
You can walk through everyday
God will make the crooked road straight
There you will be able to enter into the gate

Through every wilderness and mountain you shall go
All of the high hills will be made low
Every rough place God will make plain
There you will be able to explain

He'll open the rivers in high places
You can rejoice through each one you face
He'll give a pool of water in the wilderness
That you will not be able to resist.

Sadie Moody
1997 ©

Isaiah 35:1
The wilderness and the solitary place shall be glad for them;
and the desert shall rejoice, and blossom as the rose.

God Is Our Keeper

He that hath the wings
of God above him,
Need no other protection near.

God alone is our keeper,
We have no need to fear.

God give us a calm repose in Him,
He keeps danger out of sight.

That we may lie down in peace,
As he watches us day and night.

Sadie Moody © 1997

I will both lay me down in peace and sleep,
for thou Lord, only makest me dwell in safety.

Psalms 4:8

I Cried Many Tears

I cried many tears, I can't cry anymore;
Because of the hurt and pain I just wouldn't let
go,
Discouragement came from people I knew;
Encouragement came from a very few,

Some tried to pull my character down;
And wanted me to turn around,
God will not let me fall,
Because, He's in the midst of it all

He's the one in control,
Therefore, I can always stand bold;
Just knowing Him for myself,
He's greater than anyone else.

cc:2008 Sadie L. Moody

I Cried Many Tears

I cried many tears, I can't cry anymore;
Because of the hurt and pain I just wouldn't let
go,
Discouragement came from people I knew;
Encouragement came from a very few,

Some tried to pull my character down;
And wanted me to turn around,
God will not let me fall,
Because, He's in the midst of it all

He's the one in control,
Therefore, I can always stand bold;
Just knowing Him for myself,
He's greater than anyone else.

cc:2008 Sadie L. Moody

Trust God and
Overcome Anxiety

Go to God in prayer and confident
Allow Him to guard
your heart and mind
In every situation always be content
In Him peace will surely find

Keep your mind on God
as never before
Let your belief and
sincerity be evident
Rejoice in Him forever more
It does not matter to what extent

Sadie V 1009 - 1908

Be careful for nothing, but in everything be prayer and supplication
with Thanksgiving let your requests be made known unto God
And the peace of God, which passeth all understanding, shall
keep your hearts and minds through Christ Jesus

Philippians 4:6-7

Deacon

It's Time To Resort To The Solitude Of The Mountains And Pray

While in meditation, silent petition and prayer;
There is no doubt, God will meet you there,
Communion with God will ennoble the
Character of your life
Release from your heart envy, jealousy, and strife.
In order to receive spiritual refreshing;
Continue seeking God until you receive his blessing.
We should always take the time and be set apart.
Be honest sincere from the depth of your heart.

So be ready in the morning, and come up in the morning to Mount Sinai, and present yourself to me there on the top of the Mountain. And no man shall come up with you, and let no man be seen throughout all the mountain, let neither flocks nor herds feed before that mountain.
Exodus 34:2-3

CC Sadie Moody
2/2010

44

It's Time To Resort To The Solitude Of The Mountains And Pray

.While in meditation, silent petition and prayer;
There is no doubt, God will meet you there,
Communion with God will ennoble the
Character of your life
Release from your heart envy, jealousy, and strife.

In order to receive spiritual refreshing;
Continue seeking God until you receive his blessing.
We should always take the time and be set apart.
Be honest sincere from the depth of your heart.

So be ready in the morning, and come up in the morning to Mount Sinai, and present yourself to me there on the top of the Mountain. And no man shall come up with you, and let no man be seen throughout all the mountain, let neither flocks nor herds feed before that mountain.
Exodus 34:2-3

CC Sadie Moody
2/2010

Your Struggle Is Over

If you are struggling with a broken heart
God wants to restore and give you a fresh start

Your past and present hurt may be holding you back
God is ready and willing to make it alright

From my experience, I know how you feel
I also know God can restore and heal

Even when you don't understand
Put it all in God's hands

Whatever you do always do your best
And, then allow God to do the rest

Luke 21:19 "In your patience possess ye your souls"

Ce: 2009

Sadie L. Moody

God will not Fail Thee

When you try and don't succeed
Just seek God and take heed
Continue trying again and again
The battle is hard but you will win

Many times you may fail
Hold on to God and you will prevail
It's no disgrace when you strive
God is the answer to our every lives

Sadie Moody
© 1997

Deuteronomy 31:8,

And the Lord, he it is that
doth go before thee; he will
be with thee, he will not fail thee,
neither forsake thee; fear not,
neither be dismayed.

A Strong Soldier

A very very strong soldier you are
You've kept the faith thus far
Continued steadfast in the Lord
When the battle was very hard

You believed God would bring you out
Trusted Him and did not doubt
You stood very strong
When it seemed all was going wrong

Many couldn't see nor understand
But you knew what God had planned
Always calling on God in prayer
Knowing that He would meet you there.

Sadie Moody
©1998

I Peter 5:10

But the God of all grace, who
hath called us unto his eternal glory
by Christ Jesus, after that ye have
suffered a while, make you perfect,
stablish, strengthen, settle you.

Be Careful What You Say

When ugly words are spoken against a person,
It can cause much hurt and pain;
Because once you have spoken them,
They may never feel the same;

The same as a knife, they can be cutting,
Most time not even true, they were said because you were mad,
But, you act as though you really said nothing;
If you never meant to say it, you wish you never had.

Words sometimes spoken in haste,
Especially when they are not true;
They can never be erased,
And it's something you cannot undo.

Be careful about the words you say;
When a person is hurt, it's hard to go away,
So, whoever you stated your words to;
They will always remember they came from you,

Pray and think about what about what you say because, lies and ugly
words can cause GOD's precious chosen one to go astray.

Proverbs 17:4 - A wicked doer giveth heed to false lips; and a liar giveth ear to a
naughty tongue.

James 3:14,15 - But it ye have bitter envying and strife in your hears glory not, and
lie not against
the truth, this wisdom descendeth not from above, but is earthly, sensual, devilish.

Sadie Moody /cc: 2009

Desires of Your Heart

Obey God's commandments in

the fullness and not in part,

He will meet every need

And give you the desires of your heart

Rest in Him in all you do

There's nothing He will withhold from you,

Trust him and obey

He will certainly make a way

Sadie Moody
© 1997

Deuteronomy 11:24
"Every place whereon the soles of your feet
shall tread shall be yours;
from the wilderness and Lebanon,
from the river, Euphrates,
even unto the uttermost sea shall your coast be."

Desires of Your Heart

Obey God's commandments in

the fullness and not in part,

He will meet every need

And give you the desires of your heart

Rest in Him in all you do

There's nothing He will withhold from you,

Trust him and obey

He will certainly make a way

Sadie Moody
© 1997

Deuteronomy 11:24
"Every place whereon the soles of your feet
shall tread shall be yours;
from the wilderness and Lebanon,
from the river, Euphrates,
even unto the uttermost sea shall your coast be."

There Is Hope

My trust is in you Lord
For all you've done for me
The matter may sometimes seem hard
But my hope is yet in thee

Psalm 39:7
And now, Lord what wait I for? My hope is in thee.

Sadie L. Moody
© 1998

Mary, Mother of Jesus
"Blessed Among Women"

Mary, the Mother of Jesus was put on this earth
Among many women, one of the most blessed
Many couldn't see nor understand
But Mary knew what God had planned

Mary was spiritual, humble and most pure
Her dedication to God was sure
Very powerful and strong around
In her life no sins were found

She had no wealth nor acclaim
But her living Holy was not in vain
Among the history of many women she was unique
The life she lived will forever speak

Sadie Moody
©1998

Luke 1:28

And the angel came in unto her and said, Hail, thou that art highly favoured, the Lord is with thee: blessed art thou among women.

Fruits of the Spirit

Symbolic Biblical Meaning
Of The Apple

This fruit was used figuratively to show how precious we are to God, and how extremely sensitive he is to our needs.

Proverbs 25:1
A word fitly spoken is like apples of gold in pictures of silver.

The Fruits of The Spirit

Love

Faith

Joy

Goodness

Peace

Gentleness

Longsuffering

Love your friends and enemies as well
Joy and happiness when everything fails
Peace when there's confusion in your midst
Longsuffering when tests and trials yet exist
Gentleness when you've done no one wrong
Goodness towards the one that does you harm
Faith to believe it's all in God's hand
The fruits of the Spirit will always stand

Sadie Moody ©1998

Galatians 5:22
But the Fruit of the Spirit is love, joy, peace, longsuffering, gentleness, goodness, faith.

The Symbolic Biblical Meaning Of The Olive Tree

The best oil was obtained from the green olive fruit. It was used as anointing oil, and for dressing wounds.
The most famous olive garden mention in the bible is Gethsemane, meaning "Oil Press"

Matthew 26:36
Then cometh Jesus with them unto a place called Gethsemane, and saith unto the disciples,
sit ye here, while I go and pray yonder.

CC: 2010
Sadie Moody

The Symbolic Biblical Meaning Of
The Olive Tree

The best oil was obtained from the green olive fruit. It was used as anointing oil, and for dressing wounds.
The most famous olive garden mention in the bible is Gethsemane, meaning "Oil Press"

Matthew 26:36
Then cometh Jesus with them unto a place called Gethsemane, and saith unto the disciples,
sit ye here, while I go and pray yonder.

Symbolic Biblical Meaning
Of The Melon

Restoring of the soul; refreshened; Fruitfulness

Isaiah 3:10
Say to the righteous, that it shall be well with them: for they shall eat the fruit of their doings.

Fruit For Food
And Its Leaf For Medicine

And by the river upon its bank, on this side and on that side, shall grow all trees for food, whose leaf shall not fade, neither shall its fruit be consumed; it shall bring forth new fruit according to its months, because their waters issued out of the sanctuary; and it's fruit shall be for food, and it's leaf for medicine.
Ezekiel 47:12

CC 2010
Sadie Moody

61

Fruit For Food
And Its Leaf For Medicine

And by the river upon its bank, on this side and on that side, shall grow all trees for food,

whose leaf shall not fade, neither shall its fruit be consumed; it shall bring forth new fruit

according to its months, because their waters issued out of the sanctuary:

and it's fruit shall be for food, and it's leaf for medicine.

Ezekiel 47:12

C.C. 2010
Sadie Moody

Symbolic Biblical Meaning

Of Grapes

Grapes symbolize abundance and prosperity.

The Fruit of the vine symbolized Jesus' shed blood.

Jesus referred to himself as the vine and to his followers as the branches.

Symbolic Biblical Meaning Of The Pomegranate Fruit

The pomegranate is a symbol of the resurrection and the hope of eternal life. Because of its abundance of seeds, it can also symbolize royalty and the church, where the seeds represent the many believers who make up the one universal church.
It's also among the pleasant fruits of Egypt

The Lord thy God bringeth thee into a "good land"
Verse 8– A land of wheat and barley, and vines and the fig trees and pomegranates; a land of olive oil, and honey
Deut. 8:7-8

CC 2010
Sadie L. Moody

Symbolic Biblical Meaning Of The Fig

Jeremiah used the fig tree as a symbol of "desolation". It also signified security and hope.

Desolation: Left alone, forsaken.

King Hezekiah was afflicted with boils, Isaiah cursed by applying a poultice of figs. Figs have a drawing affect.
II Kings 20:7

I will surely consume them, saith the Lord: there shall be no grapes on the vine, nor figs on the fig tree, and the leaf shall fade; and the things that I have given them shall pass away from them.
Jeremiah 8:13

CC:2010
Sadie L. Moody

The Glory of the Lord

The Glory of the Lord

When God's glory comes into our midst,
We'll know that His spirit does exist
As a light proceeds to and fro
Deliverance will come as we know.

His spirt shall come upon thee
All sickness and diseases must flee
In our minds we'll have no doubt
Because we'll know what it's all about

His Glory is in our midst

© Sadie Moody 1997

Haggai 2:9
The glory of this latter house shall be greater than of the former,
saith the Lord of host; and in this place will I give peace, saith the Lord of hosts.

Isaiah 60:1
Arise, shine; for thy light is come, and the glory of the Lord is risen upon thee.

God's Servants

Our Keeper

God Is Our Keeper

He that hath the wings
of God above him,
Need no other protection near.

God alone is our keeper,
We have no need to fear.

God give us a calm repose in Him,
He keeps danger out of sight.

That we may lie down in peace,
As he watches us day and night.

Sadie Moody ©1997

*I will both lay me down in peace and sleep,
for thou Lord, only makest me dwell in safety.*

Psalms 4:8

God Gave Me a Vision
Of
Our Future Together

I saw the things that were to be
People didn't understand nor did they see
We were given a lifetime love
Not from men, but from God above

I can remember when our love was new
Words of encouragement came from a few
Through all of our ups and down
Our marriage is built on solid ground

God gave five witnesses through visions
It wasn't left to others and their decisions
Being ordained by God it came to pass
When God is in control it will surely last

Sadie L. Moody
cc: 2001

71

Music

Anointed
Music

M - usic played

U - nder the anointing ushers the

S - pirit down upon us

I - n such a great way it

C - auses many to feel God's
presence and be healed

73

Minister Of Music

One who plays and ushers in the anointing
And the spirit of God come upon us
As the anointing enters our midst
The spirit of God does exist.

Music brings on peace and calmness to our souls.

Mother's Day

The Mother of Faith

Even before the birth of the child,
preparation should begin.
The world is full of snares and danger that
will never end
A Mother recognizes that the child will
encounter temptation
Spiritually she tends to the molding of
character & mind in every situation.

The children cannot discern the hidden
danger
There is so much hate, bitterness and
anger.
A Mother believes God for her children
when gone astray
She stands strong in faith and fail not to
pray

Sadie L. Moody
cc:2006

The Woman Who's God's Prophetess

One whom God uses to foresee,
Of happenings that will be;
She has a true vision;
Not based upon her own decision

Words spoken come with authority & power
That we may take heed this day & hour,
A woman gifted and not intrepid,
Used by God to reveal whatever is hid

Sadie L. Moody
C: 2006

And Deborah, a prophetess, the wife of Lapidoth, she judged Israel at that time.
And she dwelt under the palm tree of Deborah between Ramah and Beth-el in mount
Ephraim: and the children of Israel came up to her for judgment.
(Judges 4:4&5)

PALM TREE-Represent Victory

The Woman Who's God's Prophetess

One whom God uses to foresee,
Of happenings that will be;
She has a true vision;
Not based upon her own decision

Words spoken come with authority & power
That we may take heed this day & hour,
A woman gifted and not intrepid,
Used by God to reveal whatever is hid

Sadie L. Moody
C: 2006

And Deborah, a prophetess, the wife of Lapidoth, she judged Israel at that time.
And she dwelt under the palm tree of Deborah between Ramah and Beth-el in mount
Ephraim: and the children of Israel came up to her for judgment.
(Judges 4:4&5)

PALM TREE-Represent Victory

Mother, You've Shown Me The Way

Mother, you've shown me the way
In which I must go
I don't know how to repay
But, regardless I love you so

The words of encouragement you've given me
Are more valuable than anything
But sometimes it's hard for me to see
I do thank you and I won't complain

Sadie Moody
© 1998

Proverbs 31:28
Her children arise up, and call her blessed.

The Mother of Faith

Even before the birth of the child,
preparation should begin.
The world is full of snares and danger that
will never end
A Mother recognizes that the child will
encounter temptation
Spiritually she tends to the molding of
character & mind in every situation.

The children cannot discern the hidden
danger
There is so much hate, bitterness and
anger.
A Mother believes God for her children
when gone astray
She stands strong in faith and fail not to
pray

Sadie L. Moody
cc:2006

The Overworked Mother

The strength of the Mother should be
tenderly cherished.
A lot of her strength is spent in exhausting of her
labor.
Her care and burdens should be nourished'
Because, in doing for others she shows no
favor.

Sometimes she may feel rejected.
In helping others they sometimes become
dissatisfied.
Her physical needs should never be neglected.
And, the wishes of the Mother should be gratified.
Sadie L. Moody cc: 2006

Acts 9:36 "Full of good works and almsdeed."

Mothers Are Precious

Mothers are precious in everyway,

They encourages you to stand today

Of all the Mothers greatest and small

You Mother are the greatest one of all

I'm so thankful for you,

For all of the wonderful things that you do.

By: Sadie L. Moody

cc: 2001

The Overworked Mother

The strength of the Mother should be
tenderly cherished.
A lot of her strength is spent in exhausting
of her labor.
Her care and burdens should be nourished;
Because, in doing for others she shows no
favor.

Sometimes she may even feel rejected.
In helping others they sometimes become
dissatisfied.
Her physical needs should never be
neglected
And, the wishes of the Mother should be
gratified.
Sadie L. Moody cc: 2006

Acts 9:36; "Full of good works and
almsdeed.".

Prophetess

The Woman Who's God's Prophetess

One whom God uses to foresee,
Of happenings that will be;
She has a true vision;
Not based upon her own decision

Words spoken come with authority & power
That we may take heed this day & hour,
A woman gifted and not intrepid,
Used by God to reveal whatever is hid

Sadie L. Moody
C: 2006

And Deborah, a prophetess, the wife of Lapidoth, she judged Israel at that time.
And she dwelt under the palm tree of Deborah between Ramah and Beth-el in mount
Ephraim: and the children of Israel came up to her for judgment.
(Judges 4:4&5)

PALM TREE-Represent Victory

Mountains to Climb

Taken in Miami, Fla.
"1986"
Fontableu Hilton

Anointed
Music

M ~usic played

U ~nder the anointing ushers the

S ~pirit down upon us

I ~n such a great way it

C ~auses many to feel God's
presence and be healed

It's Time To Resort To The Solitude Of The Mountains And Pray

While in meditation, silent petition and prayer;
There is no doubt, God will meet you there,
Communion with God will ennoble the
Character of your life
Release from your heart envy, jealousy, and strife.
In order to receive spiritual refreshing;
Continue seeking God until you receive his blessing.
We should always take the time and be set apart.
Be honest sincere from the depth of your heart.

So be ready in the morning, and come up in the morning to Mount Sinai, and present yourself
to me there on the top of the Mountain. And no man shall come up with you, and let no man be
seen throughout all the mountain, let neither flocks nor herds feed before that mountain.
Exodus 34:2-3

CC Sadie Moody
2/2010
Sadie Moody

89

God Made Mountains to Climb

The stumbling blocks placed in your way
Are just a step of victory each and every day.
Sometimes you may get tired of fighting it all,
Each time you try, the more you fall.

You even say to yourself, "Why struggle today?"
I'd rather give up, That's the easy way.
So, before you think about giving up the next time
Just remember, God made "Mountains to Climb."

Sadie Moody © 1998

God is our refuge and strength, a very present help in trouble.
Psalm 46:1

Your Season

Your Fiery Trial

Think it not strange,
When you go through a fiery trial,
It does seem very hard,
But, it's only what God has allowed.

They sometimes comes behind each other,
It makes life feel,
You can't go any further,
But God is right there by your side.

Your Struggle Is Over

If you are struggling with a broken heart
God wants to restore and give you a fresh start

Your past and present hurt may be holding you back
God is ready and willing to make it alright

From my experience, I know how you feel

I also know God can restore and heal

Even when you don't understand
Put it all in God's hands

Whatever you do always do your best
And then, allow God to do the rest

Luke 21:19 "In your patience possess ye your souls"

Cc. 2006
Sadie L. Moody

93

It's Only For A Season

That's what you're going through right now
You really don't understand the reason
But rejoice in the Lord anyhow
Because it's only for a season

Remember it's not in your hands
Cast everything out of your mind
Because God said he's in command
In Him peace you will surely find

That's the Reason,
It's Only for a Season

*To every thing there is a season, and a time
to every purpose under the heaven:
Eccles. 3:1*

Soon Coming King

God Is Declaring Judgment To This Rebellious Nation

Injustice is festering and so is greed
And people haven't taken heed
Businesses are blooming and boundaries are bulging
There's more and more sins people are indulging

True worship has been replaced with hypocritical religious motions
God desires our entire life and not just a portion;
He's trying to mobilize this nation to repent;
That we may visualize the nearness of his judgment

In this world there is so much contesting,
Many people all over this world are stressing
God's Prophet cries out for righteousness and justice
In order that the people may receive peace

Famine, floods, drought and plagues are going to bring us to our
knees
Because of the directions this nation is headed, God is not pleased
Remember, God always send a prophet who lashes out at sins
unflinchingly
One who speaks with power, authority and intensity

Amos: 3:1—6:14

Sadie Moody [cc:Feb. 2011]

FRET NOT GOD IS WITH THEE

Fret not because of the evildoer
One day they will become the battle losers
They walk to and fro day by day
Biting against you in every way

Within their heart lies envy and strife
The words they speak cut as a knife
Sowing discord is one thing God hate
You will not be able to enter His gate

Some falsely accuse you with all their might
Knowing a liar shall not tarry in God's sight
The seeds they sow will come back around
Faint not, God will take care in due time

Psalm 21:11-For the intended evil against thee: they imagined a
mischievous device, which they are not able to perform.

By: Sadie Moody
Cc2001

God's Chosen Deacon

Commissioned by the Apostle as he laid hands
He has the reputation of a good man
Full of wisdom and the Holy Ghost
Helps in the ministry whereever needed most

One who seeks God and really prays
Continually praying each and every day
When the Apostle preaches and the people are being fed
He's always witnessing "Amen" to God's word

He looks into the ministry spiritual oversight
That no one would be left slight
In all that he does blameless he was found
Even when no one else was around

Sadie Moody   ©2000

For they that have used the office of a deacon well, purchase to themselves
a good degree, and great boldness in the faith which is in Christ Jesus.
I Timothy 3:13

Remember Time is Valuable

Make the most of today because, time is passing by.
Treasure every moment you have.
Share your miracles and your
blessings with someone else.
To realize the value of one year, ask a student
who failed a grade
To realize the value of one month, ask a mother
who gave birth to a premature baby
To realize the value of one week, ask the
editor of a weekly newspaper
To realize the value of one hour, ask the person
who prayed for one hour
To realize the value of one minute, ask a person
who missed the train
To realize the value of one millisecond,
ask the person
who won a silver medal in the Olympics
"Time waits for no one"
Yesterday is history
Tomorrow is a mystery
Today is for sharing time
Share your valuable time and be blessed.

Sadie Moody
©1998

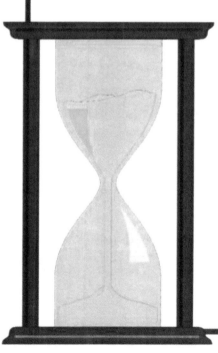

100

Rejoice

Yield To The King
(Y2K)

The year of 2000 Y2K is almost here
And the end of time is approaching near
Many are troubled about the future event
But God wants us to relax and be content

Remember, God is the one in control
He only knows what the future holds
Surely we may face a difficult test
God is still over the whole universe

So, as the Spirit of God moves in our midst
We'll know certainly God still exists
So yield to the King as never before
Because soon, these days we'll see no more

Sadie Moody © 1999

*Now, be ye not stiff necked, as your Fathers were, but yield yourselves unto the Lord, and
enter into his sanctuary, which he hath sanctified forever: and serve the Lord your God,
that the fierceness of his wrath may turn away from you.*

II Chronicles 30:8

101

Yield To The King

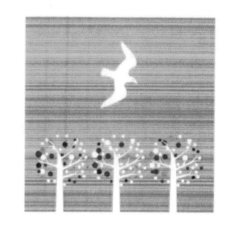

The year of economic crisis is almost here
And the end of time is approaching near,
Many are troubled about the future event;
God wants us to relax and be content,

This world is drowning in discouragement and uncertainty;
Many have lost control of their destiny,
There is hope in discouraging times;
God is going to turn things around.

Remember, God is the one in control;
For He knows what the future holds,
Surely, we are facing a difficult test;
God is yet over the whole universe;

So as the spirit of God moves in our midst;
We know for certain God still exists,
So yield to the King as never before;
Soon these days we will see no more.

cc:2007
Sadie Moody

"Now, be ye not stiff necked, as your Fathers were, but yield
yourselves unto the Lord, and enter into his sanctuary, which
he hath sanctified forever: and serve the Lord your God that
the fierceness of his wrath may turn away from you."
II Chronicles 30:8

On Your Journey

As you journey away from home,
Always remember you're not alone;

Whenever you're going through a test,
Remember always put God first;

Allow Him to guard your heart and mind,
In Him, peace you will surely find;

Hoping your journey be blessed and safe,
As you enter into a new place;

May God keep & bless you in all that you do,
For our prayers are with you;

I will never leave thee nor forsake thee.
Hebrew 13:5b

We Love You!
Humbly Submitted:
The Moody Family

The Gossiper

Always telling something you heard
Saying they said, he said, she said, and it said
Not knowing the truth about the matter
But with your lips they always flatter

Stop being a talebearer, and strife will cease
Because God requires all of us to follow peace
When lying on others, it causes ruin
Conversation that's not of God, we should shun

Hating on others causes strife;
Ugly words spoken cut as a knife,
Be careful what you say or do,
Because God's seeing eyes are watching you.

The words of a talebearer are as wounds, and they go down into the inner most parts of the belly.
A lying tongue hateth those that are afflicted by it; and a flattering mouth worketh ruin.
Proverbs 26:22,28

Cc: 2009
Sadie L. Moody

Minister Of Music

One who plays and ushers in the anointing
And the spirit of God come upon us
As the anointing enters our midst
The spirit of God does exist.

Music brings on peace and calmness
to our souls.

Minister Of Music

One who plays and ushers in the anointing
And the spirit of God come upon us
As the anointing enters our midst
The spirit of God does exist.

Music brings on peace and calmness
to our souls.

Printed in the United States
by Baker & Taylor Publisher Services